The Giant Bathroom Book of Cartoons

The Giant Bathroom Book of Cartoons

Magpie Books, London

Constable & Robinson Ltd
3 The Lanchesters
162 Fulham Palace Road
London W6 9ER
www.constablerobinson.com

This edition published by Magpie Books,
an imprint of Constable & Robinson Ltd 2007

A copy of the British Library Cataloguing in
Publication Data is available from the British Library

ISBN-13: 978-1-84529-751-0
ISBN-10: 1-84529-751-2

Printed and bound in the EU

1 3 5 7 9 10 8 6 4 2

Animals

Cats are under tremendous
peer pressure to remain useless.

"It's because I'm a bull, isn't it".

4

Animals

"Well, it's similar to bungee jumping, but you go up instead of down."

Animals

"I don't like the way that rhino's preparing to charge !"

"Let's see if you qualify for a handout.
How many nuts do you have currently,
and where are they buried?"

HEY MAN, THIS IS GOOD SHIT!

Animals

"Very funny - now can you spit the water back out"

Animals

"Sure, I'm calmer. I'm just concerned the tranquilizer darts may be habit-forming."

Animals

'Vultures are renowned for their use of thermals'.

Big dogs. One of the reasons
little dogs are so nervous.

Animals

"I think he likes you."

Animals

"Mum, Dad. This is Sushi."

INSULT
OF THE DAY

I have had a perfectly wonderful evening, but this wasn't it.

Groucho Marx

JOKE OF THE DAY

Two cows were talking in a field one day.
  The first cow said: 'Have you heard the one about the Mad Cow Disease that's going around?'
  The second cow said: 'Yeah, makes you glad you're a penguin, doesn't it?'

Art

Art

"For goodness sake Miss Pendleton,
stop jiggling about!"

Art

"It's fabulous! I'll give you £25,000 for it!"

Art

"I'm sorry Miss, but your artistic license
has expired."

Art

"Err... The exhibits are this way dear."

"I'm a minimalist."

"We have yellow ochre, but no mediocre.
Maybe you misunderstood the teacher."

Art

"An art forger? How dare you! I am an Henri Matisse tribute act!"

..but is it art ?

THOUGHT
FOR THE DAY

If a man is standing in the middle of the forest speaking and there is no woman around to hear him, is he still wrong?

INSULT
OF THE DAY

Any similarity between him and a human being is entirely coincidental.

Business and Work

"Business is up and down."

Business and Work

"Yes, I have your letter on my desk in front of me."

THE CHRISTMAS PARTY IS CANCELLED, BUT
AS A COMPROMISE YOU CAN STILL COME
IN AND HAVE SEX IN THE STATIONERY
CUPBOARD

"You win some, you lose some. Don't worry about it. No one's keeping score."

"WE'VE SAVED A FORTUNE RELOCATING OUR CHILDREN TO ASIA..."

"If at first you don't succeed is not
company policy, Anderson!"

"Look, I said I'd bring you the report on micromanaging. Just give me a chance."

Business and Work

"*We'll skip that rubbish.*"

"Isn't that a surveillance camera?"

"Do you ever worry you've had to sacrifice your femininity to succeed in the male business world."

JOKE OF THE DAY

A small boy came home from school and told his father excitedly: 'I've been given a part in the school play.'

'That's great, son. Who are you playing?'

'The husband.'

Dad frowned. 'Go back and tell your teacher you want a speaking part.'

THOUGHT
FOR THE DAY

How is it that 'fat chance' and 'slim chance' mean the same thing?

INSULT
OF THE DAY

She's the original good time that was had by all.

BETTE DAVIS

Children

"It's nice to see the police toughening up on juvenile crime"

Children

"I'm afraid our worst suspicions have been confirmed -
We found slug, snail and a trace amount of puppydog tail."

Children

"Only twenty-five kids? Have you considered
fertility treatment?"

" One day all this will be chores."

Children

59

"Stop kicking the back of my chair!"

Children

"Alright. Who had the last toddler?"

Children

"One day, this will all be your fault."

Children

Children

"Of course Daddy & I don't mind you pillow
fighting. As long as you wear your goverment
approved pillow fighting, helmet, goggles & pads."

JOKE OF THE DAY

A banker fell overboard while taking a cruise on a friend's yacht. The friend grabbed a lifebelt, held it up, and, not knowing if the banker could swim, shouted: 'Can you float alone?'

   'Of course I can! yelled the banker. 'But this is a heck of a time to talk business!'

THOUGHT
FOR THE DAY

Work keeps us from three great evils: boredom, vice and need.

VOLTAIRE

Christmas

Christmas

"Hello, is that the temp agency? Now listen,
I specifically asked for *Elves*!"

"I agreed to guide you. My contract says nothing about pulling a sleigh."

Christmas

Christmas

IT'S THE GHOST OF CHRISTMAS PRESENT

Christmas

'FOR GOODNESS SAKE! SLOW DOWN AND WATCH
WHERE YOO'RE GOING...'

"and I suppose you'll be working again this Christmas?"

"So I thought why bother buying lots of small ones.."

Christmas

INSULT

OF THE DAY

Before he came along we were hungry. Now we are fed up.

Computers

Computers

MODERN POST

POST MODERN

Computers

Computers

Computers

Computers

The e-merchant of Venice

Computers

'I think the computer's trying to download
something.'

Computers

"Like, hello… nothing's wrong with the software. You hit delete. If you want to answer prayers, hit send."

Computers

'YOU'VE COPIED ALL THIS OFF
THE INTERNET...'

INSULT
OF THE DAY

He has delusions of adequacy.

Death and Funerals

Death and Funerals

"I think he must have had a death wish."

Death and Funerals

Death and Funerals

"Ashes to ashes, dust to dust,
bowl to bowl."

Death and Funerals

Death and Funerals

Death and Funerals

Death in Venice

Death and Funerals

"Actually, I'm still on life support.
I just came by to do a feasibility study."

Death and Funerals

Death and Funerals

"Welcome. You're in either heaven or hell, depending on your sex."

Death and Funerals

"Was that the tea trolley or a death rattle?"

"Not to worry. If I remember correctly, the sign described it as, 'death-defying.'"

Death and Funerals

"It's a crying shame - his wife went to visit her
mother in Australia and forgot to leave
directions to the kitchen"

JOKE OF THE DAY

Did you hear about the boy who sat under a cow? He got a pat on the head.

Family and Home

"I usually wait for it to stop spinning."

"Phew! I'm bushed! I've been up all night helping the removal men clear the front room."

Family and Home

Family and Home

"Today I'd like to teach everyone the difficult task Of, how to put a new toilet roll on it's holder."

Family and Home

"How old do you think you have to be before you can visit you parents
and get treated like a grown-up?"

Family and Home

"Take no notice of her! Next time just fetch my slippers!"

Family and Home

Family and Home

"Have you chosen your bedtime story yet Tommy?"

Family and Home

"Ah, Norman. This is Mr and Mrs Pembleton, they're going to be moving into the flat above us."

THOUGHT
FOR THE DAY

Failure is just the first step on the road to success . . . or wherever.

Fashion and Shopping

Fashion and Shopping

"The tide's getting ready to go out."

"Do these plants make me look fat?"

"I'll not have whatever you're not having !"

"Police clashed with protesters again today. Witnesses say the fabrics, textures and color schemes were just hideous."

"If your name's not down...."

FASHION NURSERY SCHOOL

Fashion and Shopping

"You wished to see me, JB?"

INSULT
OF THE DAY

He has all the characteristics of a dog except loyalty.

JOKE OF THE DAY

If a train station is where a train stops
and a bus station is where a bus stops,
what's a work station?

Food and Drink

"One cappuccino coming right up!"

Food and Drink

"Well Lucky, for starters, I think the horseshoe was a bad idea."

137

Food and Drink

"Well it doesn't look like a paperweight to me, Harris."

"Oh no! Vegelanties!"

Food and Drink

Food and Drink

Food and Drink

'EXCELLENT! THIS CRAP AGAIN'

Food and Drink

Food and Drink

It isn't about what's right or wrong, but choosing what's right for you. Therapy makes shopping way more difficult.

THOUGHT
FOR THE DAY

The grass is always greener
after ten days of relentless
driving rain.

INSULT
OF THE DAY

He doesn't know the meaning of the word 'failure', but then again he doesn't know the meaning of most words.

Health and Beauty

Health and Beauty

Health and Beauty

"I shan't be in today - I'm in bed with a nasty bug".

Health and Beauty

SO THIS 'FLAMINGO DIET'...DOES IT WORK?

Health and Beauty

"Oh shit!"   "Ugh shfjittthh!"

Health and Beauty

"I'm de-toxing my bookshelves."

When he got the wrong medication, no one would own up to it. They were real good at covering their own butts.

Health and Beauty

Health and Beauty

"It's for hair loss awareness".

"It's so thoughtful of your boss to send you a card Brian."

"No one is making fun of you. You're just being overly sensitive."

JOKE OF THE DAY

Just before the Ark set sail, Noah saw
his two sons fishing over the side.
'Go easy on the bait,' he said,
'Remember I've only got two worms.'

Higher Education

Higher Education

"He's really putting that media studies degree to good use."

Higher Education

"I've just realised something! - Thirty three years he's been at university!"

Higher Education

Higher Education

"Mum, Dad, I've decided to go to University.
I want to party for five years before I start work."

Higher Education

"Today: The collective unconscious..."

Higher Education

"I'm sorry, we're looking for somebody with experience."

Higher Education

Higher Education

Halfway around the
learning curve, Bob let go.

THOUGHT
FOR THE DAY

Against boredom, even the gods struggle in vain.

NIETZSCHE

History

"Wow! - Is that the new Pipe-x 176 Z series mobile phone?"

'Bay-owulf'

History

History

"It appears to be some sort of tax cut promise."

"It's another toga party."

BUT DR JOHNSON, OF WAT YUSE WIL
THIS DICSHUNARY OF YOURS BE?

History

History

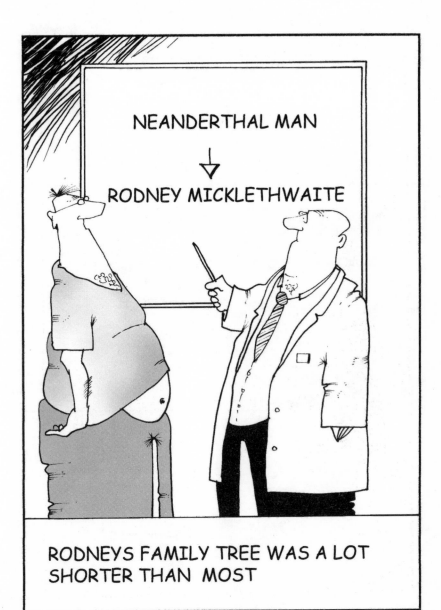

INSULT

OF THE DAY

He is the same old sausage, fizzing and sputtering in his own grease.

HENRY JAMES

Home Improvement

Home Improvement

"Peter says all these decorating programmes have given him a marvellous idea!"

Home Improvement

Home Improvement

Home Improvement

"Errr... could I see your qualifications again, Mr. Barker?"

"Sorry we've run out of sandpaper but this does a very similar job."

Home Improvement

Convenience, security and a whole lot of fun. Power windows for the home.

Home Improvement

"No, I've changed my mind again,
it looked better over there."

Home Improvement

"He came to help me pick out a pattern that I won't just get tired of after 30 or 40 years."

Home Improvement

Home Improvement

JOKE OF THE DAY

A Californian man has invented a robotic parking attendant. He's calling it the Silicon Valet.

THOUGHT
FOR THE DAY

Law of conservation of confusion: the total amount of confusion in this world remains constant. It just gets shifted around.

Law and Order

Law and Order

"Bit the wrong guy."

Law and Order

"OK, I'll read you your rights once more, but then it's lights out, no more talking 'til morning or your lawyers are present."

203

Law and Order

"Oooh - a Valentines card. I wonder who it's from?"

Law and Order

"Your nails look much better. But that wasn't why I slipped you the file."

"Now that's what I call organised crime."

Law and Order

"Tails it is. We find the defendant guilty."

Law and Order

'COULD YOU STEAL THAT ONE, IT'S ON A DOUBLE YELLOW LINE'

Law and Order

Law and Order

HE'S UPSET BECAUSE THE FRAUDSTERS WHO
STOLE HIS IDENTITY GAVE IT BACK...

Law and Order

' DON'T STOP THAT THIEF !
IT'LL BE TOO MUCH PAPERWORK '

Law and Order

"I've heard some lame excuses in my time,
but 'I'm only 7' takes the cake."

INSULT
OF THE DAY

She is such a bad cook that she uses the smoke alarm as a timer.

JOKE OF THE DAY

A man walked into a pub and saw a gorilla serving behind the bar.

'What's the matter?' said the gorilla, realizing he was being stared at. 'Have you never seen a gorilla serving drinks before?'

'It's not that,' said the man. 'I just never thought the giraffe would sell this place.'

Media

"Ok, now let's get one of you demanding your privacy."

Media

Media

Media

IT'S A BLOOD CURDLING NOVEL ABOUT THE BRUTAL MURDER OF A PUBLISHER WHO REJECTED A BOOK ABOUT THE BRUTAL MURDER OF A PUBLISHER...

"It's that idiot reporter again from the National Enquirer."

THE THERAPY DID HELP YOUR HUSBAND FIND HIS INNER CHILD... UNFORTUNATELY HIS INNER CHILD IS CALLED DWAYNE.

THOUGHT
FOR THE DAY

Collaboration is essential: it allows you to blame someone else.

INSULT
OF THE DAY

She has the sort of charm that rubs off with tissues and cold cream.

Military and War

Military and War

"Oh no! Not this again ... "

"Possible security breach, sir. It's the smart bombs. They know too much."

"Nice going. That was one of our guys, just trying to clean out the gutters."

Military and War

THE BIN WAS KICKED OVER AT 3am
THERE IS NO EVIDENCE OF TERRORIST
INVOLVEMENT, JOHN STOKES BBC NEWS

JOKE OF THE DAY

A Zen Master walked up to a hot-dog seller and said: 'Make me one with everything.'

Modern Technology

Modern Technology

FOR SAFETY REASONS WE RECOMMEND
THAT YOU USE TRADITIONAL RINGING
TONES WHEN PROGRAMMING YOUR PHONE

Modern Technology

Modern Technology

"Unfinished business used to mean going back as a ghost. Now, thanks to the Web, you can work from here."

Modern Technology

Modern Technology

Some just ain't cut out for wind farmin'.

Modern Technology

THOUGHT
FOR THE DAY

I live in fear of not being misunderstood.

OSCAR WILDE

INSULT

OF THE DAY

I have nothing but
confidence in you.
And very little of that.

GROUCHO MARX

245

JOKE OF THE DAY

A man called over to his neighbour one morning: 'Did you hear me thumping on the wall last night?'

'Oh, don't worry about it! We were making a fair bit of noise ourselves.'

Money

Money

Money

FRIDGE MAGNATE

"Damn! Telephone banking."

Money

Money

"Can I have a receipt?"

Money

"I like to keep a few pictures of my loved ones on my desk."

THOUGHT
FOR THE DAY

If you can't make yourself feel better, the least you can do is make someone else feel worse.

Movies

"We're going to have to cancel the light sabre duel, Darth-
unless you've got two AA batteries you could lend me."

Movies

"...And the best product placement in a film award
goes to..........."

261

'...we can only pay you $20 million for your next film — video piracy is killing the film industry'

Movies

Winner of the Worst Slogan Contest.

THE UNUSUAL SUSPECTS

"Oh, no! Count Dragula!"

INSULT
OF THE DAY

You take the lies out of him and he'll shrink to the size of your hat; you take the malice out of him, and he'll disappear.

Mark Twain

Music

Music

Music

"Used to sing the blues. Started popping Prozac and lost everything."

"Hurry Doctor!
This man has Saturday Night Fever!"

Music

"Those '70s flashbacks scare the Bee-Gees-us out of me."

JOKE OF THE DAY

Why did the escaped convict saw the
legs off his bed?
    He wanted to lie low.

THOUGHT
FOR THE DAY

The best time to do
nothing is whenever and
as often as you can.

INSULT
OF THE DAY

If you see two people talking and one looks bored, he's the other one.

Politics

"What are your comments on press intrusion "

Politics

286

What they'd say if they really wanted the women's vote.

Politics

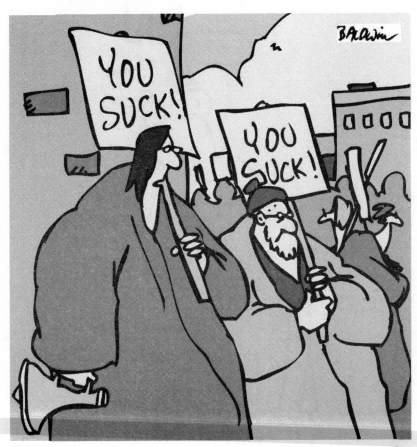

"'Establish political equilibrium through balanced representation' wouldn't fit."

"Of course as part of our ethical foreign policy the 20 kiloton population fragmentation bomb is only available to respectable governments."

INSULT

OF THE DAY

Some cause happiness wherever they go; others whenever they go.

Relationships

"Smirking or Non-Smirking ?"

Relationships

"What do you mean? Let's get undressed and
make love? I am undressed."

Relationships

Relationships

Relationships

"If we weren't married this would be romantic."

"The phone number is her idea. I think she wants to split up."

"Ha-ha – two can play at your game. You've thrown all my clothes out, so I've come back and thrown all yours out!"

Relationships

She left him to go find herself.
It only took 20 minutes, which was sort
of embarrassing, so she decided to
hang out at the mall for a while.

303

"I want to divorce my husband he's having an affair next week!"

JOKE OF THE DAY

Did you hear about the psychic dwarf
who escaped from prison?
    The newspaper headline read: 'Small
Medium at Large.'

THOUGHT
FOR THE DAY

Never underestimate the power of human stupidity.

INSULT

OF THE DAY

He has all the virtues I dislike and none of the vices I admire.

WINSTON CHURCHILL

School

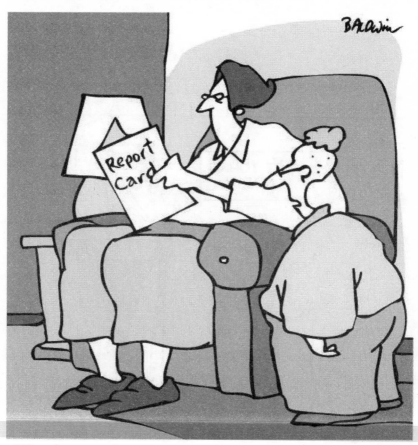

"Perhaps I possess the kind of wisdom
that only comes with age."

School

BEFORE WE DO THE REGISTER..CAN ANY OF YOU
TEACH ENGLISH?

"I'd appreciate it if you'd wait until school to do that. We've worked long and hard to bring you state-of-the-art home theater."

School

"May I remind you that my core worth as a human being remains constant, and isn't tied to external validation."

"Very impressive. Leave it with me.
Mommy will get back to you by the
end of the week."

THOUGHT
FOR THE DAY

It's a dangerous dog that doesn't bark.

INSULT

OF THE DAY

I regard you with an indifference bordering on aversion.

ROBERT LOUIS STEVENSON

Science

Science

Science

GODDARD-

'...and the award for best new-comer goes to..."

Science

Scientific Research Centre practical jokes

"My parents split up when I was very young."

"Our scientists say it would be a public health hazard, but market research shows it would sell like hot cakes - what do you think?"

Science

"Thats it. We've taken this genetic engineering too far"

Science

EUREKA...IT'S THE 'NATURAL' FLAVOUR WE'VE BEEN LOOKING FOR

INSULT

OF THE DAY

That woman speaks eight languages and can't say 'no' in any of them.

DOROTHY PARKER

JOKE OF THE DAY

What do a lawsuit and a viola have in common?

Everyone is much happier when the case is closed.

Space and Aliens

Space and Aliens

"Amazing Buzz! These moon rock samples you brought back in '69 contain evidence of water on the moon."

"Blimey, I thought <u>I</u> had a bad commute."

Space and Aliens

"I gave the human specimen some nourishment
and he blew a raspberry at me."

Space and Aliens

"I was expecting something a little more advanced."

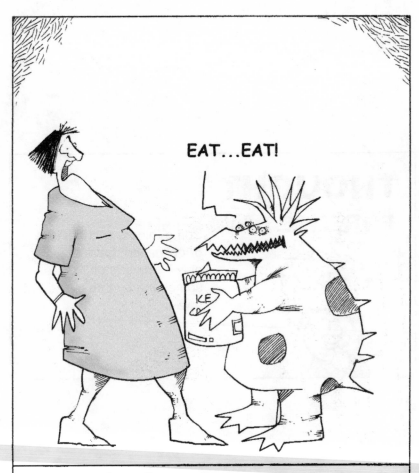

GREAT EXCUSES NO. 964

" I was on my way to the gym when I was abducted by an alien from the planet Snarg who took me to their ship and force-fed me choc chip ice cream "

THOUGHT
FOR THE DAY

Some things, such as love or obligation, have meaning only if one stands to lose something by throwing them away.

INSULT
OF THE DAY

He hasn't an enemy in the world, but all his friends hate him.

JOKE OF THE DAY

A hole has appeared in the ladies' changing rooms at a local sports club. The police are looking into it.

Sports

Sports

"I've been like this since I got back from
my skiing holiday!"

"Thanks, we really appreciate this.
Yeah, the middle button. Don't worry,
it's auto-focus – just aim and shoot."

"It was a mercy killing. I just couldn't stand to see him suffer in front of that TV each time his favorite team lost."

Sports

" *The hare's demanding a dope test.* "

356

"I second the motion!"

INSULT
OF THE DAY

Some people don't hesitate to speak their minds because they have nothing to lose.

JOKE OF THE DAY

A plane was delayed for nearly an hour on take-off. When it eventually took to the air, the passengers asked the flight attendant the reason for the later departure.

'Well,' she explained, 'the pilot was worried about a noise he heard coming from one of the engines and it took us a while to get a new pilot.'

THOUGHT
FOR THE DAY

Other people are quite dreadful. The only possible society is oneself.

OSCAR WILDE

Television

Television

Television

Television

"It's just toast I'm afraid, I've been
watching cookery programmes all evening."

365

Television

Television

Television

"Move! You're blocking the TV."

Television

INSULT
OF THE DAY

He was a tubby little chap who looked like he had been poured into his clothes and forgotten to say 'when'.

P. G. WODEHOUSE

JOKE OF THE DAY

Two nuclear physicists got married recently. The ceremony was beautiful – she was absolutely radiant, and he was glowing, too. Even the bridesmaids shone.

THOUGHT
FOR THE DAY

One fool may maketh many.

Travel and Tourism

"Does my bomb look big in this?"

Travel and Tourism

Travel and Tourism

I CAN'T PUT MY FINGER ON IT PHILIP...BUT SINCE YOU CAME BACK FROM THE SAFARI YOU'VE BEEN **DIFFERENT!**

"Wait, maybe it's, 'Keep your eyes on the road and your hands on the wheel.'"

"Houston, contact a Mr. Malcolm Tadworth
of Sussex. I've found the luggage from
his 1987 holiday to Marbella."

Travel and Tourism

"You may find the mosquitos around here a little tiresome"

Travel and Tourism

THOUGHT
FOR THE DAY

The enemy of your enemy
is your friend.

JOKE OF THE DAY

Why don't actors stare out of the window in the morning?
  Because if they did, they'd have nothing to do in the afternoon.

THOUGHT
FOR THE DAY

Any fool can criticize,
condemn and complain
and most fools do.

BENJAMIN FRANKLIN

Credits

Ian Baker
14, 24, 43, 61, 76, 87, 123, 135, 143, 152, 189, 195, 228, 239, 263, 274, 304, 351, 354, 382.

Mike Baldwin
3, 7, 11, 13, 27, 41, 44, 62, 70, 77, 88, 95, 97, 99, 103, 109, 121, 124, 126, 137, 144, 153, 155, 159, 171, 192, 194, 201, 203, 205, 207, 209, 212, 218, 221, 230, 232, 240, 242, 249, 265, 273, 276, 287, 289, 298, 300, 303, 311, 313, 315, 316, 352, 355, 366, 368, 380.

Adey Bryant
5, 9, 16, 21, 25, 47, 55, 59, 64, 93, 102, 105, 110, 112, 114, 116, 117, 158, 164, 167, 175, 188, 190, 193, 204, 251, 261, 296, 299, 301, 324, 335, 339, 341, 384.

Credits

Clive Goddard
4, 10, 12, 22, 29, 36, 45, 56, 69, 71, 75, 82, 85, 94, 98, 122, 136, 150, 157, 166, 177, 187, 202, 206, 259, 272, 284, 295, 297, 305, 321, 323, 336, 338, 350, 364, 376.

Grizelda
15, 37, 42, 60, 74, 84, 86, 89, 96, 140, 142, 149, 154, 156, 196, 208, 211, 217, 219, 229, 250, 253, 262, 275, 363, 365, 383.

Richard Jolley
23, 26, 49, 57, 63, 101, 104, 113, 115, 163, 165, 168, 178, 191, 227, 231, 255, 260, 264, 267, 290, 325, 329, 337, 340, 375, 377, 381, 385.

Joel Mishon
6, 30, 58, 72, 81, 83, 125, 127, 129, 139, 141, 176, 180, 182, 238, 252, 266, 283, 285, 288, 302, 322, 327, 342, 349, 356, 378.

John Morris
35, 38, 40, 48, 128, 130, 138, 169, 179, 254, 326, 357.

Animals

Fran Orford
8, 28, 39, 46, 73, 100, 111, 151, 170, 181, 183, 210, 220, 222, 233, 237, 241, 243, 271, 277, 286, 291, 312, 314, 328, 330, 343, 353, 367, 369, 379.